PAUL S. SCHUDER
Science Collections

Woodland Public Library

Mimbres design from Art of a Vanished Race

Animal Ways

Animals Fighting

JANE BURTON

Newington Press

First published in the
    United States in 1991 by
    Newington Press
2 Old New Milford Road
Brookfield, Connecticut 06804

First published in Great Britain in
1990 by Belitha Press Limited

Library of Congress
    Cataloging-in-Publication Data

    Burton, Jane
    Animals fighting/Jane Burton.
Brookfield, Conn.: Newington Press, 1991.
    24pp.: col. ill.; cm (Animal ways)
    Illustrates why and how animals fight.
Includes dogs, cats, antelope, cocks,
blackbirds, crabs, fish, butterflies, beetles,
and lizards.
    1. Animal fighting—Juvenile literature.
    2. Animal behavior—Juvenile literature.
    3. Aggressive behavior in animals—
        Juvenile literature.
I. Title   II. Series
591.566

ISBN: 1-878137-03-4

Animals must have space in which to find enough food for themselves and their families. So animals often fight about space.

◄ The mute swan on the left is defending his space—called his territory. He has seen another male swan in the distance and is swimming toward him to drive him away.

Above, a male golden hamster has come to visit ▲ a female. But he is not welcome. There is a scuffle, and the female chases him out of her territory.

Some animals need a lot of space, and others need much less.

In this grain storage area there is so much food that a great many house mice can feed together without bickering. Even so, one mouse cannot help being bossy! It wants the grain of wheat that another mouse is eating. The second mouse gives up the meal without a fuss. It can always pick up another grain, so there's no need to fight.

In a hard winter food is scarce. But an apple has been put out for the fruit-eating birds. One bird finds it, eats as much as it can, and then stands guard over it. Another bird would like some too, but the first bird will not share. If other birds eat the apple, it will soon be gone and the first bird might then starve. So this bird fights all the other birds and drives them away, guarding the apple as long as it lasts.

Even butterflies can fight—but it is a rather feeble battle. ◀ The peacock butterflies on the facing page are competing for a thistle flower. They flick their wings at each other, making a clicking noise.

Shore crabs are better-armed but are mostly peaceable. ▼ The crabs on the left are using their pincers to push, not nip. At right, two soldier crabs are wrestling seriously. There is a whole beach to feed on when the tide goes out, ▼ but this must be an especially tasty patch if they have to squabble over it.

Animals need not always come to blows to keep intruders out of their territory. They have special signs that warn others to stay away.

Mammals leave smell messages wherever they go. On the facing page, a roe deer buck, or male, is marking his territory with scent from a gland on his face.

Fishes signal with their fins. The sailfin molly above is warning off a trespassing male.

Birds have loud calls and eye-catching displays. The bird above is a male bustard. He walks with feathers fluffed, advertising that he needs all this big space for himself, his mate, and their chicks.

When warnings fail, a fight starts. These bantam cocks have been strutting, clapping their wings, and crowing at each other from inside their terri- ▲ tories. Now they stand and glare at each other, beak to beak. Their neck feathers stick out like ruffs, to make them look huge and frightening. Each waits tensely for the other to make the first move.

Suddenly the buff cock leaps into the air and ▲ slashes downward with his sharp rear claws, or spurs. The blue cock somersaults backward, slashing up to defend himself.

Now the battle rages. First one cock, then the other, leaps highest. Each tries to jump on top of the other and wound him with his spurs. Sometimes they stop and glare at each other, then leap and slash even harder. They joust as if they love fighting, and they can go on for hours.

In the end, one of the cocks tires first. The match ends when the loser totters away, back into his territory. The winner staggers after him a little way. But he is so tired, too, that he soon goes back to *his* territory to recover. They will fight again another day.

Antelopes live in herds made up of females and their young, led by a big, strong male. Young male antelopes, like the two wildebeestes on the facing page, often practice fighting as they play. But one day each will challenge an older male and try to take over a herd.

The two male antelopes on the right are impalas. They were *really* fighting. Now the herd leader is chasing the ▼ young impala away.

The two young giraffes on the left are practicing fighting in another way. They are "necking"—pushing shoulders and hitting neck against neck—which is the way that giraffes fight.

Dogs are pack animals, and males fight to be the pack leader. The top dog can grab the most food, and he can boss all the "underdogs." He leads the fight when strangers come into the pack's territory.

Brothers start scrapping when they are small. At first, their power struggles look just like play. The two dogs on ▲ the left are still puppyish. But the two on the right are ▲ nearly grown up, and their snarling match is serious. Once young dogs have settled who is strongest, that one will stay top dog. All he has to do is growl and *look* bossy.

Female dogs—called bitches—also fight. The top bitch in a pack is often even more bossy than the top male. All the others roll over on their backs to show that they know she is the boss.

Puppies often nip and snarl at each other as they tumble around in play. But they seldom hurt each other. Older dogs, like the two on the right, also wrestle and play. But when the top dog begins to snarl, the others know it's time to stop. They know better than to pick a fight—because the top dog will always win.

▲ Fighting is one of the many skills that kittens learn at playtime. They grab each other with paws and mouth, and kick and yowl. But they do not scratch or bite hard because they are only play-fighting.

Kittens tell each other it is only a game by not showing ▲ their teeth much, even when their mouths are open. But if one kitten does get hurt it says so—by baring all its teeth, narrowing its eyes, and snarling, as if in a real fight. ▶

▲ Red deer stags, or males, fight in earnest during the autumn. They wallow in smelly mud and run around their territories, bellowing a challenge to other stags. The females feed or rest, taking no notice of the uproar.

Some of the stags have no territory. At dusk ▲ they move about in a restless herd, fencing with each other. The strongest stags may go on fighting all night. They lock antlers and heave and push ▶ until they come to a standstill, exhausted. The top stag wins the ownership of the territory and all the females that live in it.

▲ These insects are stag beetles. Their "antlers" are their jaws. The jaws can bite hard and hold on tight, and they are used for fighting.

During the day stag beetles hide in cracks in old tree stumps. At dusk the males come out to look for females. When two male beetles meet, they ▲ face off, antlers to antlers. The beetles are quite big, and their movements are slow compared to those of other insects.

Stag beetle males often fight when there is a female nearby. Females, like the one in the picture ▲ on the left, have small, sharp jaws and can nip hard. But this female seems to take no notice of the struggle nearby.

When one male beetle finally gets hold of the ▲ other, he raises him high in the air. Then, with a toss, he flings him away. The losing beetle falls to the ground with a "clack."

Many kinds of fish live in pairs, and each pair needs plenty of space. Males chase out other males, first by a display of fins, then by fighting.

▼ This Siamese fighting fish spreads his gorgeous fins—ready to fight. The intruder displays back at him. If neither gives way, they will go for each other like fighting cocks. They will not give in until all their fins are in shreds.

The tiger barbs on the right beat one another ▼ with their tails in combat. Each tries to knock the other off balance.

Other fishes fight by mouth-wrestling, catching hold of the other's lip and tugging and shaking. The tussle ends with the weaker fish breaking away and turning pale to signal defeat. On the ▼ left, two fish called Jack Dempseys are in the middle of a wrestling match. But they are not enemy males—they are a courting pair.

Two fish called kissing gouramis look as if they ▼ are courting, but *they* are fighting! Sometimes they spin around together, "kissing" each other on the sides.

Index